ANIMAL MAGICIANS

Mystery and Magic of the Animal World

David Taylor

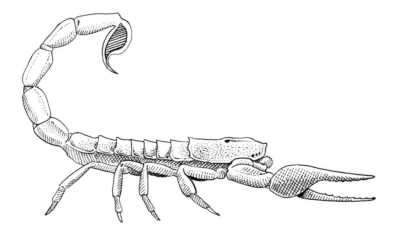

Lerner Publications Company
Minneapolis

All words printed in **bold** are explained in the glossary on page 46.

Front cover: The chameleon

First published in the U.S. in 1989 by Lerner Publications Company.

Copyright © 1988 by David Taylor.
Original edition published 1988 by Boxtree, Ltd. London,
England under the title DAVID TAYLOR'S ANIMAL MAGICIANS:
THE MYSTERY AND MAGIC OF THE ANIMAL WORLD.

Library of Congress Cataloging-in-Publication Data

Taylor, David, 1934-
    Animal magicians: mystery and magic of the animal world/David
Taylor.
        p.   cm.
    Includes index.
    Summary: Describes a variety of animals with remarkable
characteristics, including the chameleon, electric eel, bat, and
hummingbird.
    ISBN 0-8225-2175-X (lib. bdg.)
    1. Animals—Miscellanea—Juvenile literature. [1. Animals.]
I. Title.
QL49.T217 1989
591—dc19   88-36778
                                                      CIP
                                                      AC

Manufactured in the United States of America

1 2 3 4 5 6 7 8 9 10 98 97 96 95 94 93 92 91 90 89

Contents

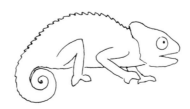

Introduction

In a special sense, all living things are magical. Though scientists and engineers have built amazing machines, such as space shuttles, computers, and lasers, they have never come near to constructing anything so intricate, so mind-boggling, and so mysterious as the simple worm or minute amoeba. There is no such thing as a run-of-the-mill animal. But there are many animals that are particularly clever and dramatic in the ways that they go about their daily business. These show-business personalities use all sorts of spectacular wizardry and theatrics. But they don't perform their tricks merely to entertain and delight audiences, as do human conjurers and illusionists. These wizards work their magic to survive.

Who invented sonar, gunpowder, the helicopter? Who discovered how to use electricity? Certainly, great scientists and inventors perfected these machines and devices. But they modeled their inventions on systems that had been developed millions of years before. Bats were using sonar, eels were using electricity, beetles were fighting off enemies with gunpowder, and hummingbirds were hovering like helicopters long before humans came up with materials and machines that could perform the same magic. Bats, eels, and hummingbirds are but a few of the creatures that delight us with their wizardry and theatrics. Let us meet the *animal magicians* and enter a world of mystery and illusion.

Captain of Firepower

Flash! Bang! Kaboom! Stage magicians often make their entrances in dramatic ways—enveloped in a cloud of smoke or accompanied by a clash of cymbals. Our first animal magician begins its enthralling act in just the same way. With a sharp explosion and a puff of billowing vapor, the amazing *bombardier beetle* makes its entrance. Bang! It fires a second time!

The bombardier beetle is actually a sort of living cannon. It is able to fire explosive charges from the tip of its abdomen. This is

A bombardier beetle fires on its attackers.

the bombardier beetle's defense against ants and other ground beetles that may try to attack it. The defense is startling and effective. Bombardier beetles are found in many parts of the world, including Africa, Asia, the East Indies, and North America. They are ground-living insects that are mainly **carnivorous.** Their diet consists of mites, spiders, flies, and other small insects. Most bombardier beetles are marked with patterns of bright and contrasting colors. One European bombardier beetle bears the apt name of *Brachinus explodens*! It is a beautiful species with brown wings and violet wing covers. Bombardier beetles are usually found under stones, in hedges, and in open woods. In India there are bombardier beetles that may grow up to 2 inches (5 centimeters) in length.

The bombardier beetle looks like an ordinary bug, but it has a sophisticated defense system.

Ready, Aim, Fire!

How does the bombardier beetle produce its artillery fire? The secret is in a gland that lies within the back part of the beetle's abdomen. This gland contains two chambers. In the inner chamber the beetle produces two chemicals: hydrogen peroxide and quinone. In the outer chamber the beetle manufactures a special enzyme called peroxidase. The explosion happens when the hydrogen peroxide and quinone pass out of the inner chamber to a special "combustion chamber." There they mix with the peroxidase and this triggers a violent and instantaneous explosion. As with many chemical reactions, the explosion produces heat. In the bombardier beetle's case, so much heat is produced that one-fifth of the chemical material is **vaporized.** The rest of the chemicals reach boiling point—212°F (100°C). The beetle sprays its target with this mixture of boiling liquid and hot vapor that smells like iodine. The insect is quite a sharpshooter and can swivel the end of its abdomen in many directions in order to hit its target with great accuracy. The spray produces a burn on human skin and can be both agonizing and dangerous if it hits a person's eyes.

Many other kinds of beetles produce distasteful or even poisonous chemicals in their bodies. Some of these chemicals are so powerful that African hunters once used them to make poison arrows. The brightly colored designs on the beetle's body serve as a bold advertisement for the unpleasant consequences of tangling with it. The patterns are quite unlike those of most harmless insects, which try hard not to be noticed and sport dull colors or even **camouflage** themselves. A **predator** that has once tried a mouthful of say, a *ladybug*, knows only too well the horrible taste. It will watch out for the distinctive, spotted red or yellow insects in the future and steer clear. The same applies to the conspicuous colors and markings of bombardier beetles. Their flashy appearance says, "Beware! Keep Off!"

Millions of years before the Chinese invented gunpowder, the bombardier beetle was firing its remarkable, self-contained cannon. A very clever little beetle indeed!

Jeweler of the Sea

Our next animal magician is a master jewel-maker! Diamonds, emeralds, sapphires, rubies, amethysts, garnets, and all of the other precious and semi-precious stones are created deep within the earth by chemistry, heat, great pressure, and the passage of time. But one jewel—and one alone—is made by a living animal. It is the pearl.

Pearls are created by shellfish—particularly by bivalve **mollusks.** Freshwater *mussels* from the rivers of Scotland and

Traditional pearl fishermen used heavy stones to help them reach oysters at the sea's bottom.

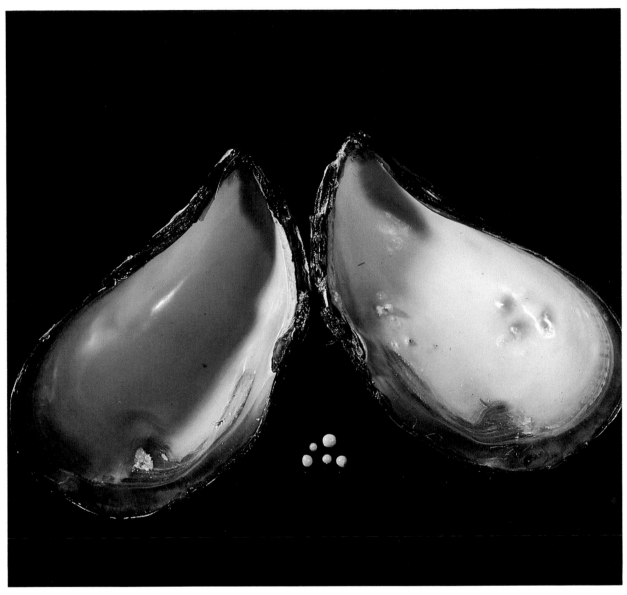

Oysters aren't the only shellfish that make jewels. Five tiny pearls came from this mussel.

Wales have yielded valuable pearls up to 1.5 inches (4 cm) in diameter. Legends say that Roman general Julius Caesar, who possessed a breastplate studded with British pearls, invaded Britain partly out of his desire for Scottish pearls.

Clams also sometimes make pearls, and the biggest pearl ever discovered, the Pearl of Lao-tze, was found in a giant clam in the Philippine Sea in 1934. It weighed over 14 pounds (6.5 kilograms) and was once valued at over $4 million.

But the master of pearl-making is the *oyster*. The *pearl oyster* is not the sort of

oyster that people eat in restaurants with wedges of lemon and brown bread. It is a completely different species. The oyster lives within a shell that it makes itself. The shell has two halves, an upper and a lower, that are joined by a hinge. There are several species of oysters and all live in warm, tropical waters. Some pearl oysters can measure 12 inches (30 cm) across and can weigh as much as 11 pounds (5 kg). But generally they are much smaller.

The oyster, however, is not just a blob of jelly inside a chalky shell. The oyster's soft tissue and hard shell are so intimately linked

This oyster from Tahiti contains a valuable silver-black pearl.

that they cannot be separated without killing the animal. Both make up the living body of the creature. The animal's mouth, stomach, heart, and nervous system are all found within the shell, as is a muscle that the oyster uses to close or open the shell. The shell also holds flat, crescent-shaped **gills** that are covered with rows of microscopic hairs. These hairs lash rhythmically in the water to bring oxygen and food (oysters eat **plankton**—tiny animals and plants) to the animal.

An Unwelcome Intruder

So what are pearls? The ancient Greeks and Persians thought that pearls were formed by drops of rainwater falling into open oyster shells. In fact, pearls are the result of an irritation, an itch, a nuisance. The pearl is the oyster's answer to an unwelcome intruder in its body. A pearl is formed when a tiny worm, a grain of sand, or a bit of seaweed finds its way inside the oyster's shell. The uninvited guest irritates the oyster and causes it to begin protecting itself by surrounding the intruder with a calcium-containing substance called *nacre*. Nacre is a lustrous, shimmering material that lines the shells of oysters and some other mollusks. It is more commonly called mother-of-pearl. Layer by layer, as time goes by, the nacre is laid down around the irritant, and this forms a pearl. If the pearl is attached to the inside of the oyster's shell, it may develop an irregular shape and have little value. Ideally, a pearl should lie free somewhere in the soft body of the oyster and should be perfectly round or pear-shaped.

Color is also very important to the value of a pearl. Most pearls are murky white or cream-colored, but some pearls may be pink, yellow, green, golden, or brown. Pink pearls are sometimes found in the great conch shell of the West Indies. The valuable black pearl is chiefly produced by pearl oysters of the Gulf of Mexico.

Japanese culturers inspect a catch of oysters and pearls.

Treasures of the Ocean Bed

Pearl fishing has been carried on for thousands of years in India and the Persian Gulf, and more recently in the South Pacific and Central American waters. Pearl oysters are usually found in shallow, inshore waters. Traditional pearl fishers in India dive for oysters with the aid of a 45-pound (20-kg) stone that pulls them down to the sea's bottom. There the divers pick up the oysters and place them in baskets to be hauled to the surface by companions. Some exceptional pearl divers have stayed under water for as long as six minutes on one lungful of air.

Over 700 years ago, the Chinese began to encourage freshwater mussels to make pearls. They gently opened the animals' shells with a sliver of bamboo and introduced an irritant such as a pellet of mud, bone, brass, or wood. The mussels would produce pearls of curious shapes after a period of up to three years. Pearls formed in the shape of the divine Buddha were particularly highly prized. In the late 19th century, the Japanese advanced the art of **culturing** pearls and discovered how to manufacture spherical (perfectly round) pearls. Culturers insert a bead of mother-of-pearl into the body of an oyster. After the operation, the oyster is returned to the sea for about seven years before it is finally opened for the extraction of the pearl.

Because pearls are largely composed of calcium, they dissolve in acid solutions. It is said that Cleopatra, the queen of Egypt, once dissolved a pearl in a glass of wine. The pearl was said to be of more value than the whole of the banquet she had provided in honor of Mark Antony. Cleopatra then drank the wine after toasting Mark Antony's health. The next time you see a humble mussel or clam washed up on the beach, remember those master jewelers that so impressed the court of the queen of Egypt.

Prince of the Orient

Every theater needs a superstar, especially one with a reputation for mystery and intrigue. As the curtain rises to a haunting oriental tune, out of the wings shuffles the *giant panda* with its characteristic rolling gait.

The giant panda, the mascot of the World Wildlife Fund, is one of the world's least known and most endangered animals. The Chinese have given the animal several names including "large bear-cat" and "he who eats copper and iron."

Giant pandas, it seems, have only lived in China. Their fossils have never been found anywhere else. The giant panda is now found only in western China along the eastern edge of the Tibetan mountains.

There was once a pygmy panda, but this animal is now **extinct**. The giant panda only came to the attention of the Western world about 100 years ago. The Chinese people have long hunted the panda for its beautiful fur. Sadly, poaching, or illegal hunting, still goes on.

The giant panda is easy to recognize. It has a chunky body—adults weigh around 220 pounds (100 kg)—with black and white markings on its fur. The panda's coat is dense and oily and provides ideal waterproofing in the damp mountain forests. Pandas live in the cool bamboo forests of China at altitudes between 4,000 and 11,500 feet (1,200 and 3,500 meters). The animal's molars (back teeth) are broad and flat—perfectly

Chinese legend tells us that the black markings on the panda's head and body come from black armbands worn during mourning.

This giant panda strolls among the bamboo forests of western China.

suited for crunching tough bamboo branches. On each of the giant panda's forefeet there is a special "thumb" used to grasp things. All **mammals** originally had forefeet with five **digits**. Some animals, such as the horse and the pig, have lost one or more of the digits over millions of years of **evolution**. Only the panda has more than five digits on its forefeet. The special thumb is formed from an outgrowth of the panda's wrist bone.

If you look closely at a giant panda's eye during the daytime, you will see that the pupil is not round like your own. Rather it is a vertical slit like the pupil of a cat. Like a cat, the panda is able to rapidly expand its pupils to take in more light and see better at night.

Are pandas bears? No—but they are distantly related to both bears and raccoons. Their closest living relative is the *red* or *lesser panda*, another delightful, much smaller inhabitant of the Himalayan Mountains.

A Chinese Legend

There is a legend in China that tells how the panda got its striking black and white markings. Once upon a time, the legend says, all pandas were pure white. One day a young girl walking in the forest came across a panda being attacked by a leopard. She at once rushed to help the panda. But in driving off the leopard, the girl was mortally wounded. At her funeral, all of the pandas in the world came to pay their last respects. As was then the custom in China, they wore the black arm bands of mourning. The pandas were so sad that they wept and wept. As they wiped their eyes with their arm bands, their eyes were blackened too. As they hugged their bodies in grief and covered their ears to block out the sound of the wailing, more black was transferred to their bodies. And, the legend tells us, they've worn the black markings ever since.

The red, or lesser, panda is the giant panda's closest relative. It looks more like a raccoon than a giant panda.

Bamboo for Survival

Giant pandas feed on bamboo shoots, which make up most of their diet. But pandas occasionally eat other plants, including wild parsnips and waterweed, and animals such as fish and small rodents. Bamboo plants come into flower once every 70 to 100 years and then they seed and die. Whole zones of bamboo forest go into flower at the same time. When these forests wither and go to seed, the giant pandas starve. In days gone by, the animals would simply migrate in search of places where the bamboo plants had not flowered. But now human settlement has reduced the size of the forests dramatically. There are far fewer places for pandas to go to search for food. In recent years, in some parts of China, large numbers of giant pandas have died. There are perhaps only 500 or so pandas alive today.

Pandas love cooked meats. After catching a whiff of roasting pork, pandas have been known to break into foresters' huts to steal the meat. In so doing they often chew on the metal pots containing the food. Pandas in captivity lick their food bowls until they are spotlessly clean. They grab the bowls with their special thumbs and often chomp on the bowl rims in order to get every last morsel of food. Perhaps it is for this reason that the panda came to have the nickname "he who eats copper and iron."

A Lazy Life

Pandas aren't very energetic. They occupy fairly small home ranges of 1.5 to 2.5 square miles (4 to 6 square kilometers) and the territories of neighboring pandas frequently overlap. During most of the year the animals live alone. They usually walk less than a mile daily and may sleep for 10 hours per day. Pandas communicate mainly through scent, sound, and visual signals. There are large scent glands under the panda's tail with which the animal marks trees and other objects. Pandas can make a wide range of sounds including moans, snorts, huffs, chirps, squeaks, and roars!

Baby pandas are born white, without any

black markings at all. Females give birth after a pregnancy that can last between 97 and 161 days. The wide variation in the length of pregnancy is due to something called "delayed implantation." This allows the development and birth of the baby panda to be delayed until food is abundant and the weather is mild. A newborn panda weighs a mere 3.5 ounces (100 grams), but the animal grows so fast that by the time it is one year old it weighs almost 77 pounds (35 kg).

The giant panda looks cuddly and friendly but it isn't! It is a powerful, shy animal that can bite like a bear, squeeze hard with its forelimbs, and lash out ferociously with its strong claws. Applause please for our Chinese star!

A giant panda feeds on bamboo shoots. Bamboo makes up most of the animal's diet.

Wizards of Energy

The next group of animal magicians will shock you. These are not talking parrots or chattering chimps that occasionally offend us with their antics. There are actually animals that have the power to give electric shocks. These animals are living batteries that were using electric power for millions of years before Benjamin Franklin began experimenting with electricity in the 18th century. Some of these creatures can knock people off their feet—or even kill them—with electricity.

All living cells, the building blocks that make up every kind of plant and animal—from the amoeba to the blue whale, from seaweed to redwood trees—produce very tiny amounts of electricity. The electricity is produced by the chemical reactions that are continually happening inside each cell. Certain cells, such as those that make up muscles, produce more electricity than others. The electrical activity in these cells is still minute, but it is great enough that doctors and veterinarians can examine a big,

A living battery, the electric eel can deliver a 400-volt shock.

The South American knifefish is constantly sending out rapid electrical pulses that help it understand its environment.

active muscle like the heart with a machine called an electrocardiograph. The electrocardiograph plots the electrical currents produced by each heartbeat. The instrument detects abnormal electrical patterns caused by heart damage or heart disease.

While humans and most animals don't produce much electricity, some fish produce high levels of electricity in surprising ways. The *knifefish* of Africa and South America and the African *elephant-snout* live in muddy water and have very poor vision and hearing. They find out what is going on around them by *electrifying* their environment. These fish have living "batteries" within their bodies that continually emit up to 1,600 electrical pulses per second. The pulses may measure 3 to 10 **volts** depending on the

size of the fish. The electricity is emitted day and night and it forms a "field" around the fish. The fish can detect any object in the water—a plant, another fish, or a stone —that interferes with the electrical field. Knifefish and elephant-snouts possess hundreds of tiny pores arranged in regular patterns all over their skin. The pores contain an electricity-conducting jelly and they serve as the fish's electrical detectors. Some knifefish live in calm waters and send out electrical impulses rather slowly—at a rate of perhaps two pulses per second. Other knifefish, which prefer fast-running, turbulent streams, need more electrical power to understand all the activity around them. They fire 400 pulses per second. Even more amazing is that some species of elephant-snouts use

An elephant-snout of West African waters. Some elephant-snouts use their electrical signals to send messages to one another.

electrical signals to send messages to one another. Scientists have recorded "songs" and even "quarrels" conducted over this fish radio! The history books tell us that Guglielmo Marconi invented the wireless radio. Tell that to an elephant-snout!

The Real Stunner

For truly shocking power, however, there are fish that can produce shocks of up to 650 volts of electricity! The *electric eel* and the *electric ray* are capable of injuring or even killing a healthy adult human by electrocution. Electric *catfish* are not quite as powerful.

All electric fish use their power for one or two of the following reasons: as a defense, to locate and obtain prey, or to navigate. Adult electric eels have poor vision. The eel's electricity allows it to find out what's going on around it in the rivers where it lives. Its electricity also acts as a formidable weapon. The electric eel is very dangerous and can deliver an average punch of 400 volts of electricity per second. It can keep this up, without its "battery" running down, for days on end if necessary. Direct contact with an electric eel can kill a person. Horses have been knocked unconscious by shocks sent through the water from several feet away. In 1941 two men fell into a U.S. Army research pool containing electric eels and were killed instantly.

Where does the eel's electricity come from? Over half of the eel's body—an adult can weigh up to 100 pounds (45 kg)—is made up of special electricity-producing cells called *electroplaques*. The electrical system can be "shorted" if the two ends of the eel touch metal simultaneously. Then there will be a

massive discharge of power that will kill the fish! Normally the electric eel catches its prey, which includes other fish and frogs, by stunning it with its electrical emissions. Eels don't actually kill their prey with their shocks because they will only eat living animals. Dead electric eels can still be very dangerous —their bodies continue to send out shocks for as long as 12 hours after death.

Electric rays, also known as *torpedo rays*, are marine (ocean-going) fish. They are sluggish swimmers that spend most of their time partly buried in the sandy bottom of shallow waters. They have blocks of electricity-producing cells that make up about one-sixth of their total body weight. The electrical organs are situated on each side of the ray's plate-shaped head. The top surface of the ray is electrically positive and the underside is electrically negative—just like an ordinary flashlight battery! Electric rays don't produce as much voltage as do electric eels, but the salt water in which they live conducts the power more effectively than does fresh water. An electric ray can deliver a punch of up to 220 volts of electricity in a series of discharges that gradually drain the animal's "batteries." Some hours of rest are needed for the ray to recharge its batteries.

Electric catfish are found in certain African rivers. They aren't very "shocking"— possessing a small electrical organ that can only produce up to 90 volts of electricity. Electric catfish tire easily and can't keep up the shocks for very long. The ancient Egyptians named the electric catfish "the releaser" because of its ability to deliver a shock. They knew that if a fisherman hauled an electric catfish in with his nets, he would receive such a jolt that he might drop the net and lose the whole catch of fish!

An electric ray is built just like a flashlight battery: its top surface is electrically positive and its bottom surface carries a negative charge.

Emperors of Light

Many thousands of years ago, primitive people discovered how to use fire as a source of light. By the 19th century, people had learned how to create light using electricity. But the magicians of the animal kingdom have been creating firework displays and illuminating the darkest jungles and the deepest oceans for *millions* of years.

All sorts of living things make light. They don't do this by striking matches, they create light *within* their own bodies. The light they create comes in a dazzling array of colors and all of this light is cold—like the light in a neon tube. Among the many animals that can give off light are certain bacteria, fungi, worms, deep-sea fish, prawns, and insects.

Luminous fish of the ocean depths light up the darkness with their own bodies.

A tropical squid puts on a dazzling light display.

Lanterns of the Sea

In the deep ocean, there are **luminous** animals, such as *dragonfishes*, that are festooned with more lights than a cruise liner on the Caribbean. Some fish are decorated with glittering yellow, purple, and green "bulbs" that hang from their bodies. Some deep-sea *angler fish* have "lanterns" of bright light dangling in front of their jaws to attract prey. There are several kinds of deep-sea fish that flash their lights at one another to communicate in a sort of fish Morse code!

The luminous shrimp, *sergestes*, is decked out like a neon sign. Green and yellow light patterns run in quick succession from its head to its tail. Luminous *squids* have very complicated lamps within their bodies. These lamps are complete with lenses, reflector mirrors, and shutters! Some squids have powerful searchlights that they use to track moving prey and to blind enemies.

Some animals generate light from chemical reactions within their own bodies. Other animals, such as the common squid, can't make their own light, but take on luminous bacteria that provide light for them. The bacteria are stored in tubes or bags under the squid's skin and act as living flashlights. The squid provides the bacteria with liquid food in return for the light they produce.

Of all the light-producing animals of the deep sea, the most amazing is the *diademed squid*. This squid has 24 lights that range in color from sky blue to snow white to ruby red.

Millions upon millions of microscopic marine creatures called *dinoflagellates* also produce light. These creatures sometimes make tropical seas shimmer at night. They give the ocean waves an eerie green or blue

A South American click beetle turns on its headlights.

Insect Energy

At night in Jamaica, palm trees can appear to explode suddenly into a ghostly light that can be seen for almost a mile. The cause of the light is thousands of *fireflies*, flying around the tree's branches, each one flashing its light on and off twice every second. This light attracts other fireflies and is an aid to mating. Fireflies are just one of many kinds of luminous beetles. Some luminous beetles, such as a species found in Burma, can flash their lights on and off together in perfect unison.

The Mexican *click beetle* produces the brightest light of any insect in the world. It carries two little spotlights on its back. Mexican women have been known to use these beetles as living jewels. They would put a few of the insects into fine lace bags and pin the bags to their dresses or wear them in their hair. Another species of click beetle from Central America sports two bright "headlights" and a red "taillight" and thus earns its nickname of "car bug" or "Ford bug."

The *glowworm* used to be very common in the English countryside and people were said to be able to read by its light. Now, because of changes in agriculture and the

glow and make dolphins appear to be wearing veils of light as they leap through the dark foam.

Glowworms flicker and sparkle among the trees.

loss of the low meadows where they live, glowworms are very rare in England. Glowworms produce light from the underside of the last three segments of their abdomens. The male insect doesn't glow, but it has sharp eyes. It can spot the female's light at a distance of 30 feet (10 m) or more and fly to her.

Fluorescent lamps only turn a fraction of the energy they use into light. Luminous beetles are much more efficient and turn almost all of their energy into light! How is this done? Many aspects of animal light making are not fully understood but we do know that most luminous creatures have glands in their bodies that produce two chemicals, *luciferin* and *luciferase*. Animals are able to turn on their lights by mixing these two chemicals together. When they do, they create quite a light show!

Lord of Darkness

The lights of our theater are turned low. The stage is silent. Look! Like a dark shadow, our next star swoops into view. Of all mammals, here is the supreme magician—prince of the night air—the *bat*. But there is no need to be afraid. The bat's performance deserves our admiring applause.

Mammals have a remarkable variety of habits and **habitats**. Many mammals live on the ground. Some mammals, like the dolphin and whale, have taken to the ocean to live among fish. Some mammals, like the mole, are specialist underground dwellers, and some mammals vie with the birds for mastery of the skies. Nearly one quarter of all mammalian species are bats—the only mammals

Cave-dwelling bats live in darkness. A sophisticated sonar system helps the bats navigate through the pitch-black cave.

Large bats called flying foxes roost in trees in Indonesia. Unlike most bats, flying foxes have excellent eyesight.

with the power of real flight. There are 951 species of bats and you have probably never heard about many of them. Among this unfamiliar assortment we find the *hammer-headed bat*, the *greenish naked-backed bat*, the *least flying fox*, the *shaggy-haired bat*, *Peter's sheath-tailed bat*, the *Egyptian tomb bat*, the *Buffy flower bat*, *Wagner's moustached bat*, and the *banana bat*.

One of the great mysteries surrounding bats is the question of how the animals evolved. We think that bats took to the air about 50 million years ago. Their ancestors are thought to have been shrewlike creatures that ate insects. The bones of the animal's forelimbs and fingers then grew enormously long and the skin between the fingers, forelimbs, and body expanded into broad wings. At the same time, it is thought, the animal's pelvis rotated backward to permit flight and its **milk teeth** turned inward to help the baby cling to its mother's fur as she hung high above the ground.

Such changes, however, could not have happened overnight. Yet, no fossils of these shrewlike ancestors have ever been found! Bats, much as we see them today, seem to have appeared out of the blue. This is one of the greatest puzzles in zoology.

Ultrasound in the Dark

Some fruit-eating bats have large eyes. They locate food with their excellent eyesight and their sense of smell. But most bats do not rely on their senses of sight and smell to find food. These bats can "see" in the dark using a different system of navigation. They find their way using **ultrasound**—beams of sound that people cannot hear. These sounds are produced by the bat's larynx (voice box). By night, bats hunt moths, flies, and other creatures with deadly accuracy. Deep caves of the southwestern United States are inhabited by bats numbering in the millions. As the animals fly about in the total

The bat's echolocation system helps it locate moths and other prey with deadly accuracy.

blackness of the caves, they never bump into one another. What an astounding system of air traffic control! How do they do it? The answer is **echolocation**, a system of ultrasound waves. The system was being used by bats and dolphins millions of years before humans began using sonar on submarines.

With echolocation, the bat sends out a stream of sound "bleeps" that bounce off targets and come back as echoes. The bat analyzes the echoes and determines what its target is, where it is, and how fast it is moving. Even the tiniest fly can be detected by a hungry bat's ultrasound system. Each bat seems to be able to distinguish its own personal bleeps from those produced by its companions. We have yet to discover how the bat's sonar system is so precisely personalized.

The bat fires off ultrasound bleeps at up to 300 bursts per second—faster than any machine gun can fire its ammunition. It's a good thing people can't hear these bleeps for they are so loud that they register a strength of 100 decibels. By comparison, jack hammers used by road construction crews make a noise of 90 decibels! Some bats send out the noise beams through their noses and others send them through their mouths. The little *brown bat* can even eat while it emits

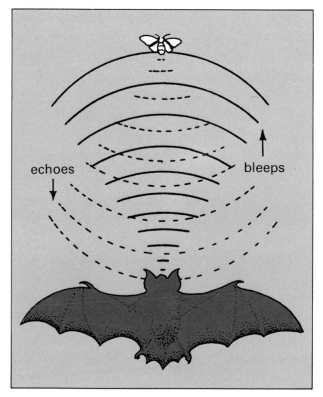

Bats send out sound bleeps that bounce off objects and prey. The bat can decipher the returning echoes.

an ultrasound beam through a special gap in its teeth. But of all bat ultrasound systems, that of the *horseshoe bat* is the most perfect. Instead of a stream of individual bleeps, horseshoe bats sometimes send out a continual wave of sound. It is the purest, most regular, and least distorted sound produced in the whole animal world. The animals must be able to recognize their fellow horseshoe bats by slight differences in the wavelengths of their individual sound beams.

Many bats have strange, often grotesque, designs of the nose and face, which give rise to peculiar names such as slit-faced, wrinkle-lipped, and leaf-nosed. These strange designs probably help the bat to direct and focus its sound beams. The bat scans the air around it with movements of the head and the ears. The *leaf-nosed bat* sweeps its head from side to side as it flies. The *greater horseshoe bat* moves one ear forward and the other back with every bleep it emits—usually around 60 per second! This ear-wagging must increase the bat's accuracy in pinpointing targets.

This leaf-nosed bat has a strange face that helps it send and receive sonar messages.

Some scientists believe the bat's sonar system is so advanced that the animal actually "sees" sound images in its brain as clearly as we see the world around us with our eyes.

Some night-flying insects have developed defenses against the bat's sonar system, just as military aircraft have developed ways to avoid enemy radar in wartime. Some insects have a soft, sound-absorbing outer layer of skin that doesn't send back clear sonar echoes. Other insects go in for fancier counter-measures. Many moths, such as the *tiger moth*, have special sonar-detecting "ears" built into their waists. When these moths realize that they are being scanned by a marauding bat, they either drop to the ground like a stone or perform complicated aerial maneuvers. The bat counters the first ploy by predicting where the moth will land and taking a shortcut to intercept it. In the second case, the bat will try to catch the insect by netting it with its wing. Certain moths have even developed ultrasound systems of their own. Once a moth detects that it is under attack, it sends out its own ultrasonic beam from a device at the top of its third pair of legs. This beam warns the bat of the moth's bitter taste. The bat then generally swerves away and goes in search of other, less ingenious fliers. Isn't that just pure magic?

Marvels of Disguise

Theater without costumes and makeup just wouldn't be theater! Only the most clever costumers and makeup artists could turn Eric Stoltz into a deformed child in *Mask* and a giant insect in *The Fly II*. Costume and greasepaint give an actor the outward trappings of a new character.

Our theater of animal magicians is no less talented. In the next act we shall see a cast of characters that, over millions of years, have mastered the art of disguise as a means of survival and success.

One of the main purposes of the color and design of an animal's skin, fur, feathers, or scales is their use as camouflage. Camouflage is particularly important among creatures

There are two kinds of peppered moths, light and dark. Each kind specializes in blending in with its environment.

A lappet moth pretends to be a beech leaf. But will a bird or another predator see through this clever disguise?

that are frequently hunted. The spotted coat of the deer fawn helps camouflage the animal as it lies motionless in the underbrush, trying not to be noticed. The speckled skin of the trout makes the fish difficult to spot against the many colors of the river bottom. Even some animal hunters, such as the leopard and the tiger, use camouflage effectively. But some animals go in for disguise in an even bigger way.

Now You See It, Now You Don't

Consider, for instance, the *moths*—insects that mostly fly by night and rest during the day. To avoid being gobbled up by birds and other predators as they doze during daylight hours, moths frequently display a wing design that allows them to blend into their surroundings and makes them almost invisible. When the russet-colored *lappet moth* arches its forewings over its body, it looks like a dry, curling beech leaf. The black and white markings of the *pine hawkmoth* give the insect excellent camouflage in the evergreen forests where it lives. The mottled and banded wings of the *brindled beauty moth* break up the animal's outline so it can't be seen against a lichen-covered tree trunk or stone. When

Can you find the buff tip moth in this picture?

29

the *buff tip moth* folds its wings together, it looks just like the broken end of a twig.

Perhaps the most fascinating of all the camouflaged moths is the *peppered moth*, once called the "pepper and salt moth" because of the black speckles on its pale cream-colored wings. This moth often rests inconspicuously on tree bark and lichen-covered stones in the English countryside. About 140 years ago, a darker form of the peppered moth appeared in the north of England. With its brown wings, the darker moth was better able to hide on the smoke-stained walls of the mills and factories of industrial towns. As industry spread in England, so too did the darker peppered moth. Nowadays the paler pepper moth is more common in the countryside where it has a better chance of survival. The dark variety does best in town. This interesting moth has given us a chance to see evolution and the process of **natural selection** at work.

Clever Costumes

But the real masters of disguise are animals that use more than clever patterns and colors in order to survive. The bodies of some animals are not only decorated, they are *shaped* to look like something they're not. Some animals mimic other animals. The *sabertooth blenny*, for instance, looks just like the harmless *cleaner fish*: its shape, design, color, and swimming style are the same. Larger fish, thinking the sabertooth *is* a cleaner fish, allow it to approach. Then, the sabertooth charges in for the attack!

The *shrimp fish* disguises itself to look like *part* of another animal—the spine of a

Strands of seaweed? No, the astounding sea dragon is trying to fool you.

This Malaysian leaf insect has a clever disguise that will fool its predators.

sea urchin. The shrimp fish possesses a long, pointed, needle-like body, and it hides, head down, among the sea urchins—safe from its enemies. As far as predators are concerned, the shrimp fish is just another prickly sea urchin spine. Other fish pretend to be plants. The *sea dragon* of Australian waters is a kind of sea horse. The sea dragon is festooned with long green tassles that make it look just like seaweed! The *Sargassum fish* of the seaweed-choked Sargasso Sea is also shaped and colored like ragged fronds of seaweed.

On land, the most specialized masters of concealment are the *stick insect* and the *leaf insect*. These creatures have bodies that are constructed and colored to look exactly like the twigs and leaves of the plants on which they live. They can stay absolutely immobile

There are three stick insects in this picture. Can you spot them?

for long periods, attracting no attention and "invisible" to any enemy.

Stick insects, or "walking sticks," are long and slender. Unlike most insects, many stick insects do not have wings. Some Asian species can reach over 12 inches (30 cm) in length. In Asia, certain stick insects are popular pets. They are easy to feed on a diet of ivy, lilac, or privet leaves. The Oriental stick insects come in colors varying from green to shades of brown. Green stick insects cannot change color, but the brown ones change regularly to blend with their surroundings. They become paler by day and darker by night. The color change is due to movement of pigment granules in the insect's skin. The granules can cluster together to make the insect appear paler or spread out toward the skin's surface to make the animal darker.

Many species of stick insects reproduce without any mating between male and female insects. The female stick insect lays eggs from which emerge small females that resemble their mother. This type of "virgin birth" is called **parthenogenesis**. In some species, such as the *prickly stick insect* of New Zealand, it is possible that males do not exist at all! Certainly nobody has ever found one yet.

Leaf insects belong to the same family as stick insects. But their bodies, by contrast, are broad and flat and have "veins" that resemble those of leaves. Their limbs possess paper-like extensions that look just like broken pieces of leaf.

Unsuspecting Victims

Most leaf and stick insects are **herbivores**. The *praying mantis* is a carnivorous insect that uses disguise not only for its own protection, but also to hide from the prey it hopes to capture. The mantis resembles a twig and has large eyes with which it can spot a victim at a distance. The insect is able to remain motionless for a long time and will wait patiently for the opportunity to seize some unsuspecting beetle or butterfly with its fast-moving front legs. Each species of mantis may have a brown and a green variety. As you might expect, the green insect is usually found among living plants, the brown goes hunting among dead plants.

Many other animals—birds, reptiles, amphibians, and mammals among them—also use camouflage in order to keep out of trouble or to help them catch their lunch. But none go to such great lengths as do the tricksters of the insect world.

This mantis hopes that its prey will mistake it for a twig.

Weavers of Illusion

Our next act takes the art of disguise even further. Once again we are going to be deceived by masters of natural magic. As the curtain rises the stage is filled with performers . . . or is it? Where are the performers? Are they still in their dressing rooms? Have they disappeared?

There is no need to worry. Although the stage looks empty, the performers are there. But each is a brilliant animal magician specializing in illusion. While the leaf insect, the lappet moth, and the Sargassum fish have clever disguises, they are born with only one costume and cannot change it. Some stick insects, as we have learned, can actually change color to match their surroundings. But there are other animals that can perform even more amazing costume changes within their own skin.

Some of these magicians not only change color, they go one better by changing their skin patterns as well. You may say that humans, too, change color. It is true that humans sometimes turn pale when they are sick, blush when they are embarrassed, or tan when they go out in the sun. But these

This chameleon has changed its costume to blend in well with a leafy branch.

color alterations are nowhere near as clever, versatile, or quickly reversible as the tricks that animal magicians can perform.

Stick insects become paler or darker, depending upon the amount of daylight, in order to blend better with their surroundings. Many other creatures, including frogs and some flatfish, can do the same thing. But the champion color changers in the animal kingdom are the *cephalopods* (the octopuses, squids, and cuttlefishes) and some lizards— particularly the *chameleon*.

Color is Skin-Deep

The chameleon is a remarkable lizard. Its eyes, which are set in little turrets, can swivel independently of one another. It can shoot its long tongue far out of its mouth to catch insects. A sticky blob of mucus on the end of the tongue helps the chameleon capture its prey. The chameleon also has a curly,

prehensile tail used for grabbing hold of things. Chameleons are found mainly in Africa and on the island of Madagascar off Africa's eastern coast. There are also a few species in southern Europe and the Mediterranean region. Chameleons are generally green in color but they can turn quite quickly to brown or another color. Flashy patterns of spots and stripes may also appear and disappear quickly on the chameleon's skin.

For an insect-hunting chameleon, the ability to adjust its camouflage quickly is a great advantage. But the chameleon doesn't just change its color for purposes of camouflage. The chameleon may display certain colors or patterns to attract a mate or to show its feelings. How does the chameleon do it? As with stick insects, there are special cells containing granules of color pigment in the chameleon's skin. The granules can spread out toward the surface of the cell and increase the depth of the skin's color, or they

This chameleon impersonates a branch. Chameleons don't change colors just for camouflage. Sometimes the lizards change colors to attract mates or show their feelings.

can cluster closely together to make the skin appear lighter. The movement of the pigment is controlled by the chameleon's hormones, nervous system, and body temperature. What is more, the chameleon's pigment cells are themselves sensitive to light and may change in response to the light around them. You might say that, to some degree, a chameleon can see with its skin!

The cephalopods—the *octopuses*, *squids*, and *cuttlefishes*—are the real show-offs of the animal kingdom. These animals are capable of extensive and speedy color changes— invaluable devices for attack or defense. Sometimes waves of color sweep rapidly over the cephalopod's body. Within seconds the animal can totally alter its appearance. These creatures carry little sacs of color pigment in their skin. The sacs have elastic walls that are attached to tiny muscles. When the muscles contract, the sacs and the pigment within them are stretched into thin discs that make the color spread widely across the animal's skin. When the muscles relax, the sacs contract and the area of pigment shrinks. Most cephalopods have three different colors of pigment—yellow, red-orange, and brown-black—often set at different layers in their skin. The skin also has little reflector cells containing chemical crystals. These crystals reflect light—allowing the animal to display another color—white. The reflector cells also **refract** light to produce green and blue effects on the cephalopod's skin. It is the various combinations of the color pigment sacs and reflector cells that create the wide variety of patterns and colors available to the cephalopod. At birth an octopus has only about 70 pigment sacs in its skin. But as the animal gets older, it becomes more skillful at color magic. A full-grown octopus has between one and two million pigment sacs.

An octopus, squid, or cuttlefish changes color not only to suit its environment, but also to suit its mood. A *common octopus* will turn white when agitated. A *Pacific octopus* will change its pale purple and gray skin to a fiery scarlet when it is upset. Some cephalopods flash different colors and patterns at one another in a sort of communication code. When alarmed, they often display light and dark patches, or they suddenly break out in stripes and spots. These fascinating animals can literally talk with their skin!

What is more, the octopus's skin is still able to change its appearance for several hours after the death of the animal. The skin cells themselves remain alive during this period and, being sensitive to the light and shade around them, go on producing their ingenious visual effects. So even a *dead* octopus can perform magic!

The dangerous blue-ringed octopus hides among stones and shells—awaiting an unsuspecting shellfish.

Miracle of the Air

And now, out of the wings, in a flash of brilliant green—the next magician floats into view! Like a gleaming emerald, it hangs suspended in the air. The wires that suspend human actors when they play the role of Peter Pan aren't necessary for this performer. Up, down, forward, and backward it darts. Meet the *hummingbird*— the genius that invented the helicopter and the vertical takeoff jet plane thousands and thousands of years before humans first went up in a hot-air balloon.

There are over 315 known species of hummingbirds and there may be others that people have yet to identify. All hummingbirds are tiny creatures with glittering **plumage** and amazing flying skills. Some hummingbirds have delightful names such as *sunbeam*,

A hummingbird needs a long bill to gather nectar from large, tube-shaped flowers.

violet-ears, *puff-legs*, and *sun-angel*. The birds live in North and South America and feed mainly on small insects and nectar. No hummingbird weighs more than ¾ of an ounce (20 g). The smallest hummingbird is also the smallest bird in the world. It is the *bee hummingbird* and it is less than 2 inches (5 c) long. As you might expect, the bee hummingbird's egg is similarly minute. It weighs less than 1/50 of an ounce (0.6 g) and is about 3,300 times lighter than the heaviest egg produced by any bird alive today, that of the ostrich. The bee hummingbird also constructs the smallest nest in the bird world; it is about the size of a grape.

The hummingbird's plumage is strikingly handsome. It usually has areas of shining blue and green. The birds often have long bills that enable them to reach far inside flowers in search of nectar. Within the bill, the hummingbird has an extendable, tubular tongue that does the sucking. The shape and length of the bill vary with each species. Those hummingbirds that eat plenty of insects as well as nectar have shorter bills. Some birds pierce the base of flower petals to get at the nectar source directly. They have sharp, strong, medium-length bills. The *swordbeaked hummingbird* needs its

A rufous hummingbird hovers like a helicopter, beating its wings 80 times per second.

very long, straight bill to reach the nectar that is plentiful at the bottom of the 4.5-inch (11-cm), tube-shaped blossoms of the passionflower. The *sicklebills* have long, curved bills that are perfectly matched to the long, curved flowers that they prefer to harvest.

Bundle of Energy

The unique thing about the hummingbird is its amazing flying abilities. Of course, it can fly through the air like other birds. But unlike any other bird, the hummingbird can hover in the air and move forward or backward while doing so. This ability is perfectly suited to the little bird's eating habits. With its wings moving so fast that they are but a faintly buzzing blur, the hummingbird nimbly hovers in front of flowers and draws off the nutritious, sweet nectar. It goes from flower to flower, much like that other nectar hunter, the bee.

What is the secret of the hummingbird's talent for hovering and flying backward? It's all in the wing. Most birds' wings contain bones equivalent to the bones of a person's shoulder, arm, and hand. The moving joint

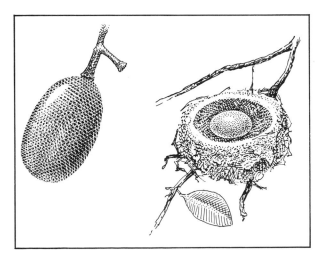

The bee hummingbird's nest is no bigger than a grape. Imagine how small the bird's egg must be.

As the hummingbird gathers nectar, it spreads pollen from flower to flower.

joint and move the wing through the air in a figure eight pattern. It is this remarkable flexibility that allows the hummingbird to maneuver its wings like the blades of a helicopter. Only *swifts*, the hummingbird's closest relatives, have a similar wing structure.

The hummingbird beats its wings at an incredibly fast rate of, on average, 80 beats per *second*! The smaller hummingbird species beat their wings even faster. The bee hummingbird may achieve 200 beats per second. Compare that with the *wandering albatross* that can glide on the air streams for many hours without even flapping its wings once.

All this wing beating means that the hummingbird uses up an enormous amount of energy. Some scientists calculate that one of these tiny birds burns about 40 times more calories per day than the average adult human! No other **warm-blooded** creature expends so much energy in proportion to its size. It is not surprising that a hummingbird must eat over half its own weight in food every day. Luckily, nectar, the sweet food used by bees to make honey, contains lots of calories and some vitamins.

The hummingbird has a unique method of saving energy while it rests at night. It allows its normal daytime body temperature of 106°F (41°C) to drop to the temperature of the surrounding air. Its body slows down as it cools, thus conserving energy. The hummingbird becomes sluggish and inert—so much so that a person can sometimes pick a bird off a branch at night as easily as if it were a dried leaf. As soon as the sun rises, however, the drowsy hummingbird comes to life and flies off to begin its busy day.

Hummingbirds are very useful to plants because they help in **pollination**. When the little bird feeds on a flower, it picks up pollen grains on its bill and face. It then transports the pollen to the next flower that it visits. Some plants have flowers that are especially designed for the hummingbird. The plants

that flaps up and down with the bird's wing is equivalent to a person's shoulder joint where the humerus (upper arm bone) meets the shoulder blade. Most of the length of the ordinary bird's wing is taken up by the upper and lower "arm" bones. These birds don't have much in the way of "finger" bones. Hummingbirds, on the other hand, have greatly elongated "finger" bones that run most of the length of the wing. The movement of the wing isn't limited simply to an up or down motion. The hummingbird can actually twist its wing at the "wrist"

that rely on hummingbirds for pollination have flowers situated well away from the leaves so that the birds can feed without becoming entangled in vegetation. Plants that rely on pollination by insects have flowers with flat "landing platforms." But the flowers from which hummingbirds gather their nectar are tube-shaped and fit the birds' long bills. Their bright red or orange colors are especially attractive to the bird's eye, but do not attract most insects.

Because of its exquisite beauty, the hummingbird has sometimes been hunted by humans. A hundred years ago, fashionable women liked to wear stuffed hummingbirds as decorations on their hats. Millions of birds were killed to make hats in Victorian times, and some of the rarest species became extinct as a result. In fact, some species of hummingbirds are only known to science because their stuffed remains came into the possession of museums. Nowadays it is the destruction of the Amazon and other jungles in South America that is the greatest threat to the survival of this most magical and charming creature.

A violet-crowned hummingbird gathers nectar from a salvia flower in Mexico.

Master of the Macabre

The lights in our theater are turned low and the stage is bathed in shadows. It is time for a spine-chilling performance. There! Something comes into the spotlight's pale pool. It advances silently and slowly— as black as night! It turns to face the audience, its claws gaping, a poisonous needle arched over its gleaming back. Spellbound, all eyes are fixed on the *scorpion*.

The scorpion has an evil reputation that is largely undeserved. Let us go and meet this fascinating animal.

Scorpions are *not* insects. Insects have six legs, **antennae**, and bodies divided into three main parts. Scorpions are *arachnids*, a class of land-living animals with eight legs, no antennae, and bodies divided into two parts. Spiders, mites, and ticks are also arachnids. Scorpions first climbed out of the sea about 400 million years ago. On land, the animals gradually developed "book lungs," leaves of oxygen-absorbing tissue that resemble pages of a book. There are about 650 different kinds of scorpions in the world.

Let's look at the brilliantly designed scorpion. Its legs have many joints and its flattened body is ideal for squeezing under things. The body has a tough protective casing or **exoskeleton**. The front part of the scorpion's body is made up of a head and chest fused

The scorpion overtakes its prey and paralyzes it with a poisonous sting.

42

Scorpions perform a strange courtship dance. Occasionally, the female scorpion devours the male after mating.

into one **cephalothorax**. The back part of the body includes the scorpion's segmented abdomen and tail. The cephalothorax is covered by a shield that has one pair of eyes in the middle and three to five pairs of eyes at the sides. The scorpion's curved, pointed stinger is located at the end of its tail. The plump base of the tail contains a pair of poison glands that open near the tip of the stinger.

As they grow, scorpions have to **molt** from time to time. They crack out of their old skin and shed it completely. This process takes one to two hours and it usually happens at night.

Scorpions are at home in hot climates. Some desert scorpions only become active when the temperature reaches 113°F (45°C). These animals will become "paralyzed" with cold if the temperature drops to 68°F (20°C). However, some scorpions live in milder climates in Europe and North America, and one species is found as far north as Alberta, Canada.

The Sting in the Tail

Certain tropical scorpions, such as *Pandinus* of Africa and *Heterometrus* of India, can grow to almost 12 inches (30 cm) in length. Such giants look frightening with their lobster-like pincers (claws) and big stingers. The pincers cannot harm a person, but the sting of a scorpion produces a burning pain. The pain may persist for minutes or even hours, but the sting of most scorpions—even big ones—is rarely fatal to humans.

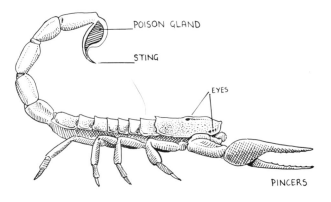

This scorpion fell prey to a black widow spider.

Even so, in North Africa and Mexico there are particularly dangerous species of scorpions. The sand-colored *fat-tailed scorpion* of North Africa delivers a large dose of nerve poison in each sting and kills a handful of people each year. Luckily, there are antidotes to scorpion poison.

Is it true that scorpions will sting themselves to death when surrounded by flames? No, it is not. Scorpions are affected by the poison of other scorpions, but the poison dosage necessary to kill a scorpion is about 200 times greater than the amount that would kill a small animal such as a guinea pig.

The scorpion is a solitary, **nocturnal** creature that hides under rocks and in crevices. In hot countries, scorpions often creep into human dwellings where they hide in beds and shoes, or under carpets. At night a scorpion will venture out to feed on insects and spiders that it grabs with its pincers and paralyzes with its sting. The scorpion feeds by tearing at its prey with its mouth, injecting digestive juices into the body of the victim, and then sucking the victim dry. Scorpions can live without food for long periods, and desert species can survive for months without water. Scorpions are fluorescent when exposed to ultraviolet light. If you take an ultraviolet lamp into the desert at night, you can see scorpions by the hundreds glowing like fiery, blue-green jewels.

Hunter and Hunted

The scorpion has many enemies and it is no wonder that it hides away during the day. Scorpions will also prey upon one another. They are also hunted by a wide variety of other creatures, including birds, large insects, toads, lizards, snakes, foxes, mongooses, bats, rodents, and monkeys. Tarantula spiders love to eat scorpions and they are immune to the scorpion's poison, as are hedgehogs. Baboons and certain nimble birds tear off the stinger before gobbling the scorpion.

Female scorpions don't lay eggs, they bear live young. The babies climb up along their mother's pincers and ride around on her back for a week or more. During this time the youngsters get along with one another quite well. After leaving their mother, however, the young scorpions become highly aggressive and are likely to attack and eat their brothers and sisters at any opportunity. From this point on, they must fend for themselves for the rest of their brief lives. Even captive scorpions, safe from enemies, rarely live longer than four years.

Although few people would call it their favorite animal, the scorpion isn't really the villain it's reputed to be. As a killer, it is no worse than a dragonfly, a leopard, or a bat. It must be its melodramatic style, its love of darkness and concealment, its fierce-looking pincers, and its unique over-the-head stab from its poison dagger that make the scorpion seem such a master of the macabre.

Baby scorpions ride on their mother's back until they are ready to fend for themselves.

45

Glossary

antenna A sense organ on the head of an insect, used for smelling and touching

camouflage Disguise
carnivorous Meat-eating
cephalothorax The front part of a scorpion's body. It includes the head and chest areas.
culture To cultivate; to produce under artificial conditions

digit A division such as a finger or toe on the limb of an animal

echolocation A system of short, high-frequency sounds that echo off objects and help animals navigate
evolution The process of change in a race or species
exoskeleton A hard outer covering of an animal's body that protects the internal organs
extinct No longer in existence

gill An organ used for obtaining oxygen from water

habitat A natural home for an animal
herbivore A plant-eating animal

luminous Emitting or reflecting light

mammal A warm-blooded animal with hair that feeds its young with milk
milk teeth Baby teeth
mollusk A member of a group of soft-bodied creatures including snails, oysters, and octopuses

molt To shed hair, feathers, horns, or an outer layer of skin

natural selection The process in nature by which those animals best suited to their environment are the ones most likely to survive.
noctural Active at night

parthenogenesis A process by which an egg develops into an adult organism without being fertilized
plankton Microscopic animal and plant life in a body of water
plumage The feathers of a bird
pollination The process by which flowering plants are fertilized
predator An animal that kills and eats other animals
prehensile Adapted for seizing or grasping by wrapping around

refract To bend light waves as with a prism. Refracted light beams often break up into colors of the spectrum.

ultrasound Vibrations with frequencies beyond the range of human hearing

vaporize To convert by heat into vapor or gas
volt A unit of electric measurement. Most flashlights use two $1\frac{1}{2}$-volt batteries.

warm-blooded Having a constant body temperature regardless of the temperature of the surroundings; able to generate its own heat

Index

Acknowledgments

Photographs are reproduced through the courtesy of Oxford Scientific Film Stills: pp. 7, 15, 22, 30, 36, 37, 39, 40, 41, 43, 44/Bruce Coleman Limited: pp. 9, 17, 18, 27, 32, 35 (Jane Burton), 10, 11 (Christian Zuber), 13 (World Wildlife Fund, Timm Rautert), 14 (Dieter and Mary Plage), 19 (Neville Coleman), 21 (Bill Wood), 23 (D. Houston), 25 (Bruce Coleman), 26 (Frank Greenaway), 29 top (Dennis Green), 29 bottom (Kim Taylor), 31 (Gerald Cubitt), 33 (Leonard Lee Russill), 45 (M. Fogden). Front cover: Dwight R. Kuhn. Other Illustrations: David Quinn.

About the author

David Taylor is a veterinarian who works with wild
animals around the world. From the Komodo dragon
to the giant panda, from killer whales to gorillas, Taylor
specializes in the problems that can beset the rare,
the exotic, and the endangered.

His adventures have been recounted in his autobio-
graphical series of *Zoovet* books and in the popular
television series, "One by One," which has been
shown in Great Britain, the United States, and many
other countries. David Taylor has recently retraced
Hannibal's epic journey across the Alps—with ele-
phants—and has been involved in the rescue of two
dolphins stranded in Egypt.

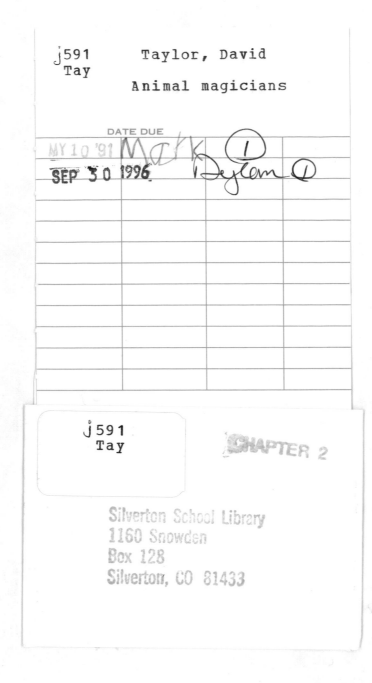

j591
Tay   Taylor, David

            Animal magicians